REBUILD

Sachiko Murakami

REBUILD

TALONBOOKS

Talonbooks
PO 2076, Vancouver, British Columbia, Canada V6B 3S3

www.talonbooks.com

Typeset in Minion and printed and bound in Canada.

First printing: 2011

The publisher gratefully acknowledges the financial support of the Canada Council for the Arts; the Government of Canada through the Book Publishing Industry Development Program; and the Province of British Columbia through the British Columbia Arts Council and the Book Publishing Tax Credit for our publishing activities.

Library and Archives Canada Cataloguing in Publication

Murakami, Sachiko, 1980–

Rebuild / Sachiko Murakami.

Poems.

ISBN 978-0-88922-670-8

I. Title.

PS8626.U72R43 2011 C811'.6 C2011-902488-8

In memory of
Yorihide Bruce Murakami

CONTENTS

Vancouver as a citytext is not the *tabula rasa* of colonialism and postcolonialism but the *tabula in absentia* of postmodernism.

—Paul Matthew St. Pierre, *Vancouver: Representing the Postmodern City*

CITYBUILD

THE FORM OF A CITY

Here, one can walk out the condo door
dressed in "clothes" known elsewhere as "pyjamas."

One can carry such debt,
one could have fed a village for a century.

Cash, no cash. Village, no village. Or village,
to village, to village, would you call this "metropolis"?

Or "New World"? Or "Pacific Rim"?
The living, "inhabitants"? "Tenants"? "Citizens"?

Eclipsed by mauve, one and one mountain.
Arms spread wide still the smallest part of enormity.

One and the other. Mountain and citizen. Part and parcel of the site.
Forgotten, already, with the first grateful sip. (How finite.)

THE FORM OF A

, can walk out the
dressed in " " known elsewhere as " ."

can carry such ,
could have fed a for a .

, no . , no . Or ,
to , to , would call " "?

Or "New "? Or "Pacific "?
The living, " "? " "? " "?

Eclipsed by , and one .
spread wide still the smallest part of .

and the . and . and of the .
Forgotten, already, with the first grateful . (How finite.)

BOUNDARIES

This is dream city, built on shores
still not ceded. This is a city of tourists
with mouths agape, these are my boundaries:
the islands in the Gulf, the sea they might call Salish,
the land taken there, taken again
from another family, that line nearly faltered.
And now a nephew with my father's grin, the last one.
Between the people and the land, what have I to teach?
To tolerate suburbs? To let the land be covered
with another's vision, then stretch our line out farther than the commuter trains,
stop where the valley's silt turns hills, the residents nearly Albertans.
The time is now, and now, and now; built so fast with minds
less changed, from Expo to Olympics,
a lifetime. More than his. Most of mine.

BOUNDARIES

dream of city, dream of built shores
dream of cedar handed over

dream of open mouths

dream of land returned
dream of descendants

dream of his open mouth
dream of the end of the line

dream of almost—
dream of his return

to ownership
to fast, faster, fastest

I AM NOT IN THE CITY

Walked out the front door again
into myth and plan, pitch and surface, and gazed
beyond the plan, always beyond it. At the bank's
front doors I lay down and wept. At the shores of False Creek
I lay down my coffee cup. Thus it was not litter.
I am thinking of running
for office. I lie convincingly
about myth, I take it for granted.
For example, the city is a wish I made
when the populace was fast asleep.
Subjected to myth, I am lost
in a maze of glass. Stalking the minotaur
sleeping at the centre. The centre. The centre.

I AM NOT IN THE CITY

The front door, the front myth and centre

pitch and surface, and centre

at the shore of False Creek I lay

in the centre

my coffee cup, my litter, my centre

beyond the plan

the centre

for office. I lie
the centre

The story invented a wish
of centre
the maze of glass. The centre

the horror

the minotaur

here

somewhere

WHERE'S THE SQUARE

Not at the centre (no centre)
Not in ocean (not without feet on ground)
Not Robson Square (not at eye level)
Not in spring (not beneath cherry blossoms)
Not City Hall (keep off the grass)

Not in Starbucks (not in that Starbucks either)
Not in Stanley Park (an on-leash park)
Not on the reserve (not Granville Island)
Not Victory Square (is it nothing to you)
Not Centennial Square (blank stare)
Not Japantown (not on current map)

PACIFIC CENTRE

Cut the city down to size and begin
again. You know what would work here?
Another development. There, there.

At its centre [Terry Fox]
I'll meet you [there]

Where the people meet [potlatch]
Where the grid ends [another grid]

Let's begin at the [ ]

Meet me at the mall at the middle of the food court

Fill me up, city and [tear me down again]

The home missing from the

Even the structure won't save you now
[another hole]

ROBSON SQUARE

no accidental usage
to make it grand
no design function

in front and
behind in
front and behind

to be seen
to sleep there
to be seen casting shadows in sleep

imagine a space
no cast
no shadows

do you know the way
to Centennial Square?
(blank stare)

is a square emptied
of name and purpose
still a square

if emptied of ice & families
then breakdancing Japanese students
then filled with ice & families

and in the bookstore, poets
mouthing through little rooms
the grandest gathering

HOLE (WEST, FACING EAST)

Size of a fist
through iris
self dugout

big as a city block
small as a condo stacked
on condo

meaning smaller and smaller
are our breathing spaces

meaning we better
think big
build more

HOLE (EAST, FACING WEST)

Build a home or a store or a tree or a library or a kiss
or a theory or a thousandth of a city

dig or fill or dug or filled or
granite or sand or fly ash or slag

or family or protest

or mortar

mortar mortar mortar mortar mortar

TOWER.

A success, a success is alright when there are there rooms and no vacancies.
—Gertrude Stein, *Tender Buttons*

A piece of grass, a peak, a peek. Whoosh and click of glass. A saddening up. A piece of self, if city. If we are to be written in account. A window means occupant, an eye. Take the elevators, please. A single suite is bland. Excess of sameness excites home. Make a decision with a mistake and then repeat until familiar. Repeat until familiar. Repeat until shat or shattered or shine or wet or sunset (always, always East) and you know, from here, West *is* East.

TOWER.

All our cadences are borrowed and foreign

Toward. To wardens. To words: untower. To top hat. To even think, *up*? To view from beyond water. To view from street (not pictured). To even think, *in*? To cluster in the green. To subordinate self to preposition. To rain-tone, to tink, *tinka tinka tinka*. To residents, this is your final notice. Towards a theory of a city: a polemic. To me you are postcard. And empty.

CONCORD HYPOTHESES

If all homes are not presales

If all master-planned communities are pre-owned

If organized into two distinct vertical columns

If the colour of urban living is coming soon

If with minimal interior common space

If the minotaur's hoof

If your time is precious

If even the smallest units have dens

If the city is built to be empty

If vacancy is an act

Then you practically touch them

(the elements (glass steel concrete

PRESALE

Consider the value.

How would you like to own an idea
that will likely change?

Consider the footprint.

I give you air, and a place to wait, suspended.
I give you the possibility of a view.

Consider the wolf.

I make you subject to change.
I write the wolf at the elevator doors.

The strategy involves actors. Especially the wolf.

MINIUM

thrown up concrete

throwing up concrete

throwing up on concrete

thrown concrete

through concrete

though concrete

thou concrete for thee

nearer   my   condo   to   thee

BOOM CRASH BOOM CRASH

Sink beyond commerce to siltish grit
and not enough history,

too much granite.

Let the realtors call, and call.

Crows in the industrial park—
mean faces, just birds.
Long before the realtors left
they were calling.

That sound? Crash. Crash. Just the waves,
still. It's a mass of water, neither housed
nor homeless.

Stand up. Spare change slips
through your fingers. Pebbles

in your pockets. Call me back. Keep walking.

CROW

I threw out that poem about the crows and the industrial park.
I was wrong about crows. They aren't metaphors for anything.
It's not just their multiplicity that's scary—though
I just wrote crow to contain the flock. Maybe Hitchcock
was reading du Maurier in bed with a handkerchief
tucked into his undershirt to catch crumbs
when he felt his fear too. In fact he was wearing a crow suit.
He was flapping around madly trying to get into the mind of a crow
so the crows in his mind would vacate the premises. He shot crows
and then held funerals his dinner guests were obliged to attend.
He carried a black quill to sign cheques with. When he sat
for a self-portrait, a crow was drawn. No, that's not it.
I drove around at sunset in an industrial park where all the city's
Hitchcocks had come to roost. A murder
of Hitchcocks flapped their handkerchiefs and threw
breadcrumbs at me. I hit the gas and drove back to town
not because I was scared but because the sun was falling
fast and it was shiny

CROW

the crows
crows

crow

I a crow
crow
crows

crow

HOLE (LOOKING IN)

What was here before?

What was here before?

TOWER ...

If I can't account for the woman missing from this city
(*the* woman, *this* city)

Imagine her life and the wholeness
that may or may not have happened

Can I mention the occupants
missing from the tower

Empty suites never inhabited
held safe for future profits

Every surface void of thumbprint
Thrum of refrigerator, lullaby, full belly

How long will they wait for life to be written
in the gleam of stainless steel

Vancouver is not a resource economy.
It is, and always has been, a real estate economy.

If the foundations are speculative
and our present is built on impatience for the future

If I can't get anywhere with Japantown
and it isn't neighbourly to mention it

If we are never living here and there is no time
to sit a minute and think at the centre

(there is no centre) near a monument
near a marker of history (there is no monument)

If we are always looking forward to the future
If my subject is not actually here

HUNT

Make fox. Make mink. Make fur with words. Make mouth full of faux. Make appearance acceptable. The fur is fake. Its warmth, real. In Montreal, summer falsifies winter, its antecedent. Itself frozen, or is warmth false? They made racetrack from mud. Made Metro. Made Expo. Made legacy of debt. Nothing from nothing. Expo shown in transport. In another city. Without drivers. Without tickets. Redundancy an impulse. Let impulse be theory. Let theory take precedent. Let's pretend. We never met. Or winter is the falsest season. November the cruellest. I never followed you through hiver. You never outfoxed me. Or were made metaphor made solid. Made real. For when fox, drag through mud. If faked fox, if dragged through snow, if the fur. If animal could choose. Its direction.

THE INTERNATIONAL PAVILION

What happens when a building built to bring together city and the world
broken by its joints and shuttled to suburb, near the river now

the crumpled bodies of trucks and dead engines.
I hear the art gallery out there is really hot.

The curator too moved from the city
Out there they're all hooked on cracked

plaster, condos built to feel urban, to feel neighbourhood
brings people together in lawsuit. I, too, am moved

Housewives mimic their children, hop the wrong way
Flipping. The wrong way.

YOU CAN RETURN HOME

Or flip it. Edge towards Pacific,
stuttering in from suburb. There,
nothing's Vancouver; plain
and river, mall and bypass.

And always the convo turns
to condo: prime plus five,
what point did you get?

What statement does your home make?
At Home Depot plants may be got
for pennies, for gardens on the starter home's
Juliette. For home, read high-rise,

for Vancouver, read Coquitlam,
for Coquitlam, read unceded Coast Salish Territory.
We grow where we're planted, in land already used,
every plot torn up and renewed.

MATERIALS

Give me something classic. Split cedar, spilled glass.
Build me a home with surfaces no one can laugh at.

I piss Paxil and Gravol, Viagra and NyQuil
into the Pacific. Salmon knows nothing of the brand. He breathes us in.

Stir coffee waste (free at Starbucks) into the ground.
Caffeine fuels me and my heirloom tomatoes, sinks into cells
that buy energy from sunlight.

One day I will claim my God-given right
to rot in the loam. Pay into the eco-market.
A stone, paid for, will mark me.

I knock on wood, trust the gravitas of granite.
Rain on pissed-on concrete. Hard and wet as home.

OCEAN VIEWS

The Pacific swells and contracts
and that's the way we like it. Visible. Breathing.
It's a necessary piece.
Its presence. For all we know

these towers are empty. Owned, and empty,
and blocking our rightful
views, which impede
the views of the tower next door.

If we are to be ruined by development,
let the rubble at least be tidy.
Let it lie far from the ocean
and views of it. Let the debris of the shores
be intentional, and thoughtful.
A seashell. A shoe. Even the shoe.
Let the shoe lie
rife with intention.

It's hard to imagine the condos
as unintentional. I can't see myself in one.
I can't afford the view. I can't help.
I can't help wanting to.

RESPONSE

Good effort, but keep the sonnet's slope within regulation limits.
This poem would work better if it had six characteristics

in common with its neighbours.
Your metaphors (of family, of home) occupy

too much lot space. Trim. Restraint is beautiful.
Buyers will be looking for restraint.

Can you integrate a big idea here?
This stanza feels "small." Too "small."

This house starts here.
No. It really starts *here.*

I feel like I've seen this before,
and I'm not sure it's for me.

HOLE (DIG IT OUT FIRST)

HOLE HOLE HOLE HOLE HOLE HOLE HOLE HOLE HOLE HOLE
HOLE HOLE HOLE HOLE HOLE HOLE HOLE HOLE HOLE HOLE
HOLE HOLE HOLE HOLE HOLE HOLE HOLE HOLE HOLE HOLE
HOLE HOLE HOLE HOLE HOLE HOLE HOLE HOLE HOLE HOLE

HOLE HOLE HOLE HOLE HOLE HOLE HOLE HOLE HOLE HOLE
HOLE HOLE HOLE HOLE HOLE HOLE HOLE HOLE HOLE HOLE
HOLE HOLE HOLE HOLE HOLE HOLE HOLE HOLE HOLE HOLE
HOLE HOLE HOLE HOLE HOLE HOLE HOLE HOLE HOLE HOLE

HOLE HOLE HOLE HOLE HOLE HOLE HOLE HOLE HOLE HOLE
HOLE HOLE HOLE HOLE HOLE HOLE HOLE HOLE HOLE HOLE
HOLE HOLE HOLE HOLE HOLE HOLE HOLE HOLE HOLE HOLE
HOLE HOLE HOLE HOLE HOLE HOLE HOLE HOLE HOLE HOLE

HOLE HOLE HOLE HOLE HOLE HOLE HOLE HOLE HOLE HOLE
HOLE HOLE HOLE HOLE HOLE HOLE HOLE HOLE HOLE HOLE

STRUCTURAL INTEGRITY

The structure is elaborate and nearing completion. The piece is nearly composed.
The city seems to be near completed. The plan is under control.
The control is developed. The usual way. The well-developed habits.
The habits are under control.

It's useful. Near completely composed.
But is the city's old plan nearly broken?
Are new habits under development? What of the usual?
Are the citizens under control?

Yes, we have developed the habit of city.
No, the citizens are not part of the plan. Unusual for us.
The development is becoming a habit.
The piece seems nearly controlled.

So, no further plans to develop the citizens.
Control is a well-developed habit. We know this.
The uses of us. The completion will signal the end of habitation.
The uses of completion. How we began to develop.
Whether the habits are worth developing. If the structure will hold.

DREAM DEVELOPMENT

I stir from a dream of Vancouver
with a mouthful of crumbling stucco. Shaken, I call
my realtor, who, I discover, has closed
his last deal and moved to Dubai
where the marina looks remarkably like False Creek.
It's intentional. Duplication. I turn and turn
and still I'm still in the same place. Dizzy, smack
against the wall. Broken bottles catch the light
and my skin. If you want to build the City
Beautiful, you need to start with quality materials
and then replicate them until beautiful. Or else
you hit the wall. You hit the wall. You hit the wall.

V6A

There is life outside of Yaletown,
and it's coming to Strathcona.

If you like it then you should put a down payment on it.
Strathcona is coming to the Downtown Eastside.

There is flexible function in Chinatown,
get at the heart of what matters most.

And look at her. I mean look at her history.
It swirls, and sputters. A distant third.

There is currently just a hole in the ground,
a wall there. Look. No. Look at where I'm pointing.

There is a different code for living.
A further bird. Missed the podium with its shit.

There is evening concierge service for your peace of mind.
Do you have a permit for that art?

There is crime prevention through environmental design.
Go for the gold.

WORK IN PROGRESS

To walk with a companion from condo to condo.
And the Yew, and the Arbutus, and the Maple
To be active, to act, to state, to inhabit this city.

To view: determined by the neighbour's rooftop.
And the Heron, and the Crow, and the Starling
To develop; to encroach; to choke.

To be a connoisseur of pebble and branch and sushi.
And Little India, and Aberdeen Centre, and Davie Street
To finish. To tarnish. To tear down—

MY WORK IN PROGRESS

I finished tarnishing. I tore down
Little India, Aberdeen Centre, and Davie Street,
became a connoisseur of pebble, and branch, and sushi.

I developed, encroached, and choked
the herons, and crows, and starlings.
But, oh, the view from my rooftop!

I am active. I act. I state. I inhabit the city
between Yew and Arbutus or Maple.
I walk with my companion from her condo to my condo.

FOR THE SAKE OF ARGUMENT

The city exists if we agree it does.
Suspend disbelief, make community.
Live in our imagination.

For the time being.
You have ten years.
The block turns, stranger.

The change becomes familiar.
The usual emptiness prevails.
A city founded on dispossession.

Vacancy made for the next generation.
Empty houses built, perpetually ready.
To be repossessed, rebuilt, resold.

MARATHON

filling in the last concrete block

and the land no longer surplus but a place to showcase

surplus to the viewers

losing momentum due to the cumulative effect of glass

on glass on glass it makes the viewer dizzy

the viewer has no access to the lost property office

False Creek sold to the wealthiest man in Hong Kong

and the viewers were flipped over his back and were soothed

False Creek was willed into existence

or—my history's a bit sketchy—

can you fill in the channel and make land

where it wasn't can you reserve a spot

at the fireworks for a different viewing

WHERE I AM

Haul in the trees, the mountains,
the ocean as far as horizon.
And piece by piece, dismantle
each Starbucks. Pack up the strip mall,
and the last of the bookstores.

If, in the middle distance,
a bus, a great big brute of a bus,
should flash by and exist there
in your field of vision,

just blink. Then cross
the street. Don't look for me.
Caught imagining, I am in

a different environment altogether.
Understand? I was never here.

HOMEOWNING

VANCOUVER SPECIAL

Not failed attempts at beauty or stating.
Unique answers to specific questions.
How may I fit my family into the equation?
How will we make the mortgage?
How much land will be allotted,
and to whom? What can't I afford?
How may we state the look
of elsewhere? How can I make myself less
abstracted? In the house but not of it.
Grace of a front lawn, stucco sophisticate.
All that glitters stuck in the surface.
Sheet shocks sense into reflection.
Wood sliced into beam better becomes
the forest. Can't see the trees for the city.
Could you move to the east? A little farther?

LET THE HOME

Let the home stand for us.

Let the beauty of our form be complex. Let our complexity be known.

A second bathroom, a fourth bedroom, sure.

But a second kitchen?

They grow like tumours in a neighbourhood organism.

Provocateurs of taste. There's nowhere to hang a metaphor.

Have you ever seen anyone on those front porches?

Is there anything wrong with letting our homes stand for us?

And still I can't get a straight answer out of anyone:

What is it that makes them so ugly?

Let the home stand.

The floor's function is to restrict and this is beautiful.

A corset on a Victorian woman.

Room to breathe is not the point.

Poor souls just living and

nothing else

VANCOUVER SPECIAL

Not failed attempts at beauty
or stating, they are unique answers
to specific questions. How can I fit
my family into my mortgage?
How can I live on the land
allotted? What *can't* I afford?
How to emulate the look
of elsewhere, to be *of*.
Grace in the form of a front lawn,
make stucco sophisticated.
All those glittering bits of glass.
Connoisseurs prefer sheets and
reflective surface, wood that recalls
wood before its felling. Once more,
this time farther east, with *feeling*.

REALTY CHECK

There is a photograph of the neighbourhood in question. I left the file on your desk. Shot from above, the house flattens into the form of the house beside it. Shot from above, the particularities of people are reduced to their scalps. This makes it easier for the invisible hand to turn the key in the bulldozer. There was no one in the room who could provide a decent answer. Then there was only rubble. No more room.

If we keep repeating the theme of the house, it will become neighbourhood. The repetition of a characteristic becomes the act of building character. They all look the same, sure, but it's a good kind of same. In holding each other, we intimate a chain link fence. Our opponents, singled out, lack vetoes. They shouldn't throw stones. The right isn't yours. It isn't mine. We dare you to step forward. To step across this line.

In order to encourage the potential buyer to close the deal, the realtor places the pen on the line she wants him to sign. The desire was already there. A person looking for a house already lives there. We do not need experts in rhetorical strategy, only cookies to bring hunger to the home. Crumbs on her lips. On her lap. Clears his voice. Whether he signs or not, she has made his refusal a choice.

VANCOUVER SPECIAL

Not failed attempt at Beauty
or indication. Unique responses
to specific questions. How can I fit
my family into the equation?
How do we make the loan?
How much land allocated and to whom assigned?
What can I not afford? How can we make do
looking like elsewhere? How do I make *me*
less abstract? Home, but not of it.
The grace of a lawn, stucco sophisticated.
All that glitters blocks the surface. Bits shock
sense, reflection. Flat wood, veneer
become a better forest. I can't see the trees
for the city. You could move a bit
"*to the east? A little more?*"

SELF SIMILAR

25 degrees 22 degrees 34 degrees **23** degrees 22 degrees 23 degrees 29 degrees
33 degrees 14 degrees 22 **degrees 38 degrees** 41 degrees 49 degrees 38 degrees
39 degrees 22 degrees **34 degrees 23 degrees 22** degrees 23 degrees 29 degrees
25 degrees 22 **degrees 34 degrees 23 degrees 22 degrees** 23 degrees 29 degrees
25 **degrees 22 degrees** 34 degrees 23 **degrees 22 degrees 23 degrees** 29 degrees
25 **degrees 22 degrees** 34 degrees 23 **degrees 22 degrees 23 degrees** 29 degrees
25 **degrees 22 degrees** 34 degrees 23 **degrees 22 degrees 23 degrees** 29 degrees
25 **degrees 22 degrees** 34 degrees 23 **degrees 22 degrees 23 degrees** 29 degrees
25 **degrees 22 degrees** 34 degrees 23 **degrees 22 degrees 23 degrees** 29 degrees
25 **degrees 22 degrees** 34 degrees 23 **degrees 22 degrees 23 degrees** 29 degrees
25 **degrees 22 degrees** 34 degrees 23 **degrees 22 degrees 23 degrees** 29 degrees
25 **degrees 22 degrees** 34 degrees 23 **degrees 22 degrees 23 degrees** 29 degrees
25 **degrees 22 degrees** 34 degrees 23 **degrees 22 degrees 23 degrees** 29 degrees

THE AGREEMENT AGREEMENT

Are you compatible with the other homes on the street?
Do you bring desirable cultural improvements to the area?

See the patterns we set: can you follow them? Are you willing to
civilize your differences? Is your character meritorious?

Do you meet the minimum requirements? Are you willing
to choose between your front yard and ours? Are you willing

to align your roof with ours? Are you willing to match our windows?
Or entrances, or porches? Is your detailing *choice*? Are your materials

choice? If we decide, will you designate your building heritage?
Will you accept our honour? Will you decline with grace?

HOW TO BUILD A VANCOUVER SPECIAL

start stucco

Clear chips of stucco, broken shards of home. Clear away debris of the long dead. Bin that shit. Heave history away. That's not ours. The tree was felled. The realtor set up the sign. The realtor removed the sign. The permit was approved. That happened right here, in a city that grows and then tears down. The land cleared where it had been cleared before. The neighbours brace themselves for the saw, the hammer. History and city hall take their toll. Now we may begin. Now that there's this hole.

start box

Here are the delineate edges, here is where inside will start. Here is the kitchen the hallway the master bedroom, big enough for six to lie prone, two for fucking, her dragged by the hair to the dirt on the ground, he hiding in the closet as though it were work, here are the beams that will hold this house up, let the hammer fall here. It falls here in its natural strike. It falls here in its natural strike. Build bigger than taste dictates. Start big, larger than the family that comes with you. For we go forth and multiply in our natural strike. For here we smooth into place laminate we will burnish with slippered feet, here we rub Formica with the oils of our hands, of garlic, of sweat, our come, here we will bleach and scour and sort the recycling. From the window we will see our patio so much bigger than the house we came from, we will see the patios lined up in the alley, so like our own, we have uprooted every bulb and spilled the seed of our countries, our runner beans wave leaves like flags, and no, no, there will be no ornamental maples on this land.

start home

Breathe gravel, unlawn. Scrub balcony, leave curtains permanently drawn. Bring suite above ground: let late autumn light make dignity for Poh-Poh, for Sheila, for laundry, for grow-op. Let box be home and let home be your own concern. Interrupt view corridors; hide Lions with maddening slope. Shrug off *ugly* and other definitions you don't control. Deflect glare. Let indignant slide off maddening slope. If neighbours sour, piss gravel. Pebble yard. Garden. *Garden.* Pick stones from gohan. Don't stir the pot. Whitewash cement lion, reach past fangs and rub smooth his stone. Clip weeds. Pour poison. Or don't.

STATUARY

The inhabitants know
what the city will and will not allow,

the lions always popular, and familiar
the sound of ocean, and gulls,

if there is unity here let me smell
your hands, your knees,

on the phone with your realtor
while the lions wait with their mouths

full of luck
you can touch

VANCOUVER SPECIAL

Enough failed attempts at Beauty
to declare, are these unique responses
to specific questions? How can he fit
a family to a mortgage?
How can he live on earth,
and what can he not afford?
What can he *not* afford?
How can he look like somewhere else?
Grace in the form, in front of a lawn in front,
our stucco sophisticated. To be. To be. To be.
All those glittering glass plates.
Connoisseurs want sheets and surfaces,
wood reminiscent of wood
before the killing. Again,
but this time farther east, with feeling.

WHERE WE STAND

Let the home stand.

The floor's function is to restrict and this restriction is beautiful.
Between walls, lithe
in their beautiful ratio, gorgeous restraint.
Our finery, our deck.

the poor souls just living and

nothing else

Let the home stand for us.

A second kitchen is not beautiful,
it speaks more of boredom than offence.
Houses that grow like tumours, their sheer size and facelessness

have you ever seen anyone on those front porches?

Our home stands for us.

In Japantown? In the rooms of billeted ESL students? (neither)

IF THE SHOE FITS

DEMOCRACY HIATUS

Homeowners!

Hoopla or civic
disobedience

An agreement broken
Doesn't feel entirely new

To change
or chance a provocation

Learning our civic lessons

Reforming our responsibility

Looking for the ruins among the ruins
that become us

Waiting for the big one to test the limits of our architecture

To witness the organizing principle

To criminalize
the witness

O LYMPIC

If you prorogue willingly or without your consent

If your spirit says something other than go, go, go

If a red mitten in the snow

If suspending democratic rights gives you a few weeks to cheer appropriately for your country

If your property is protected

If your country is represented

If this land is your land

If its citizens are

If a red mitten, no snow

If while cheering on your country you find yourself next to another citizen

If neither of you own a red mitten

If poetry is a competition

If the world is watching you on CCTV

If I am Canadian!

If this land is not my land

If the poet on the podium delivers a polemic

If you prorogue poetry for the duration of the Olympics

If your idea of spirit is complex and does not involve the nation

If you thought you were the nation

If you thought, “nation”

If you don’t

SONG OF THE CITY

The chorus improves the song.
The song improves the walk.
The walk inspires the plan.
The plan provides the city.
The city provides for its citizens.
The citizen, irreducible, and necessary.

And the chorus of glass and rained-on glass
owned by citizens, planned for, and walking
like a chorus. In a song. Of the city.

And on a walk, and humming
on the beach, in this picturesque city
full of citizens, and now a shoe.
Of a citizen? Of a migrant?
Refuge of the shore, found by a man on a walk
In a song. Of the city.

RISK

At the risk of sounding the horn, which would fell
the disobedient, the officer frowned, and the crowd
failed to disperse.

The parents considered the risk of violence
against their rights, and kept their children
well within the boundaries
of the zone designated for free speech.
Then they all became criminals.

They wanted to sound the horn.
It might fell the disobedient, disperse certainty.

The crowd failed to disperse,
outrage itself at risk. And still the officer waiting
for outrage to disperse, for the risk to be left untaken.

I manage to be on opposite sides of the country
for the Olympics and the Summit. Someone suggests
I have a natural instinct to flee bullshit. I try to organize
my anger, its definite edges.
Everything becomes abstract, and deflates.
I can be charged with wearing a disguise.

Hoopla alight, flames licking at the heels.
Poll stations empty. Now there's no one
to answer to. And spring?
No more of all that, all that violent blooming.
The shadow beneath a different mask, come true.

CIVIC CLAIMS

I am making a postulation of the city. I am making
an assumption that there is a city between the forest
and the ocean. The city is postulating me within it.
I am making a claim for the house. This one, so much
like that one. The claims. I am making claims that
have been made before but they seem
new, to me. I am demanding a claim on the city.
I am taking the city for granted. For the homes are at risk.
There are assumptions about the city that I can make.
There are these claims about the risks and I am making them.
I am sure of this. I am sure that these claims are my own.
I am making these claims because the claim is a prerequisite
to speak. I think. I am thinking about the city. These are my
thoughts about the city, and I am thinking through them.
I'm not going anywhere. I am in another city already
but the claims I make are in this present. This present:
2010, from another city, and the claim is about a house.
A certain type of house. Its relationship to the city.
I am making claims about the relationship of the house
to the postulation of the city. It's this one. This one right here.
My right to witness. The absence of the criminal.

ASHORE

Yes, we scrutinize flotsam, but the shoe remains a mystery despite how furrowed brows. Our cartwheels through language mean nothing where beach meets feet. No words. Pang of recognition. A foot, afoot. When we *a ha*, the skeleton unfuses in the mind, the drift farther afoot. The foot's adrift. That's how we got this far. Eyes roll, words loll and sink offshore despite the Internet's calm waves of information: *bzz, bzz.* We resettle into nest blot out white noise city poem. And then the bee in the room: in winter? In Google? Lazily, lazily. Another poet's called dibs on deep-sea creatures, but what sounds human at that depth? What might glub, glub mean or at that pressure, would sound sloop and slow to wrap around a jittered tongue? This foot is relevant: I want to be of sound … Prattle and throng, foot and shore, *a hoosh, a ha.* Is it right to say we are not keepers of lore, may we now screech a text? I can't remember what wail feels like. Can't forget the rules of grammar. Today we are not speaking. Type, titter, trail off, flarf. *Bzz, bzz.* Lost in our labour. Not fish but jetsam. Not keepers but bees.

THE LAST WATERFRONT PROPERTY

No scandal on Olympic land. No theft on stolen scandal. Say first we were here then define *we*. Sift midden. Whose bones, whose refuse and this is what we are refusing: no solutions to stolen scandals. First shoes then feet then all drift is suspect. Say more land on Olympic solutions. Put your foot down. No final scandals. No cost overruns on reclaimed waterfront. No reclaimed waterfront on stolen scandal. Stolen millions set adrift keep saying *scandal.* Get the storeys up and scaffolded, dig sand out and call it condo. Call castle village, village scandal. Fill village with Olympic dream and call Pacific false, call False Creek real, call your realtor, call me on this. Please. Call me on this.

WHERE YOU ARE

There is a shoe.

Awkward with the distance that comes
with contact with anything with

more substance than seawater

a shoe   a foot
or its idea
lapping at shoe, out of place
getting nowhere, another one getting
nowhere

There is a tower.

Beyond the surface, hazy with rain
and steam
from bodies unseen

A life at eye level with the street
still protected with reflected glass

There is real life that happens.

If life is more solid
in the tower than the shore

If it is transparent
If you can almost actually see—

This is where real life happens.

Combing the beach you can look up
to the towers and see nothing
but mountains between them

RETURN HOME

REBUILD

After the unimaginable, what's left: a return to rawness.
The land cracks and swallows. The home,
erased. All knickknacks back to dust. If only

that happened. Instead a neighbour
buys the bicycle, paints it blue. Instead
the graveyard markers are tactfully removed.

Instead names are changed, a farm's,
and the official memory. Now a child born in exile.

Now he becomes a father. Now redress.
Now he's a father, a body. Now ashes.

Now begin.

Now begin again.

NEARING WINTER

Having lost interest in the changing of the seasons

Having no interest in identity politics no matter how lucrative the grant

Having lost my ability to dance through verb

Having little to nothing to say about blackbirds

Having fewer than fourteen lines in me

Having lost perspective on the line break

Having handed over my neural direction to science

Having said so little and spoken less

Having the curtains finally hung, left them closed

Having the light come through of its own accord

Having sharp autumnal light

Having little interest in it beyond a spark that sputters

Having lost interest in the changing of seasons

RETURN HOME

I want to return to the home   that doesn't   call for me
nostalgia   please call me   for dinner   the house's
inward limits   clustered   his body

where it   was for   was   it for   not
        dad   it's me   you can call me

home

call me home   call me   home   call me   call me home   call me
        home call me   call me home   call me   home   call me

call me home

                    call me

                                home   call me

RETURN, HOME

As if nothing came before me.
We broke ground together.

No memory before
street and avenue.

Sculpted concrete
stroller's gentle bump

Suburb sculpted
round the ravine I was kissed in.

On our roof, a sprinkler.
On theirs, the son: pissing.

An ambulance. Another
spectacular Thursday night.
Somnambulance.

Did this happen, here? Did this
really happen to me?

MOVING DAY

The box was half-full
and the shit I threw in it never filled it, quite.
This box the sign of migration,
of tenants and the trials of uprooting,
fullness does not become it. No pretty packing chips
to bolster and protect the property. Pots and pans
rattle against cutlery, empty, enduring
hunger's din. His chequebook, our meeting's
last address scribbled with an uneasy hand. Filling up
the hungry ghost will not do. He eats forever, never satisfied.
Let's try: the official redress, rolled up, not hung
ever on the walls of the home
he didn't own: chronic renter, the family his debtor.
All property of ghosts. To the home he could not return to
his kin swell, hoard earth, buy back more
than the land that was taken. What's left for me:
poker chips, piggy banks of pennies I lugged
clear across the country where I am building,
building, building. Stacks of them, sick scent
of dirty copper that dragged him under.
I'll build towers of it, develop the landscape of desk.
A city of my own assembly, the coins of my father,
two for his eyes, a thousand more that add up to nothing,
offer no respite from rent for me or him.

M I A

a a u
a i I i i i ui
i i mi ra i
a a ria u r i
u m i r a ki i
r a r r r a a
a a ai u r m uri
u r i i u k, ur m i
a a r ri i a u a a i i u
u r i a r r, r a i i .
r : i ia r r , r u , u
r a m
i ; r i r, ami is r.
A r r m u ur
i ki ar ar u a m r
a l nd th t w s t en. Wh t's left fo e:
po e ch ps, p ggy b n s of penn es l gged
cle c oss the co nt y whe e b ld ng,
b ld ng, b ld ng. St c s of the , s c scent
of d ty coppe th t d gged h nde .
ll b ld towe s of t, develop the l ndsc pe of desk.
c ty of y own sse bly, the co ns of y f the
two fo h s eyes, tho s nd o e th t dd p to noth ng,
offe no esp te f o rent fo e o h

SPECTACULAR LOSS

Fathers are often lost in more spectacular ways:
freeway heart attacks, short-haul, faulty planes,

eggs the wrong side of three Sundays, too quick in the pan.
Mine got up to—what? Take out his teeth? And fell

at the foot of his bed, and was still, and waited
three long weeks (so the coroner says) until we

crept, guilty, through the house that spelled
disaster at its centre: the beloved

fish floating in a dirty tank,
cat shit on the carpet, the flies on every dying plant.

I took too short a look, then fled; my sister stayed on
and stared, and stared, and for weeks he came

clawing back through the dark to rouse her. He is more quiet
in the dreams. I bellow him back into being and the life I wanted him to have.

And the ashes, the last parts of him
rode with me across the continent to where he'd not been

since he hawked electronics to feed his family and his ego,
though I can't imagine far from the route he drove

from store to store, scotch mints and talk radio
and a curse rising in his throat against some new injustice.

There is no direct route to recovery except through cliché
of time healing the wound he ripped open in my vision,

all that red sadness seeping out, no light getting in.
No light at all.

MORTGAGE

My family has no trust in the bank that promised
its trust and then sold land off to neighbours, the lowest bidder.
And still they make the dead pledge,
and buy and sell without remorse, and are bought and sold:
and the deal dies when the owner does or payment fails.
Here in the lost property office we are counting
titles, dreams of picket fences tallied and accounted
and then filed away. To die with empty hands, to die a renter
in a city of homeowners, to die in a land mostly owned
by the state, to die and be buried in a little plot and become
again the land that will be bought and sold;
not even the highway will bend to your little will.
Commuters will drive to their homes far from the city,
over you, you will be under concrete, under loam. Far from home.

MO GAGE

mi ha no ru he ba ha romise
ru he so to ne bo he we bi de
he make he de ge
bu se wi ho remo se are bo a so
he de he he o ne do pa me
He he pe o we are ti
ti re pi ke ta te
he wa To wi ha to di a rente
a home ne to a mo o ne
he tate to be buri a lo a be me
gain he ha wi be bo so
no he hi wa wi be to yo wi
mute wi ri to he home ro he
o yo yo wi be de rete de ro home.

I TAKE MY FATHER TO VIEW A CONDO

Will this one do, with its views,
with its shadows? Are there
doors enough to close on me?

On your behalf I sign this document.
On your behalf, the mortgage. There's only a
dim hope of ever paying it back.

Locks changed. That day, was it sunny, was it cold?
Can I artfully say *the fish were dead?*

The flies unmaking the man.
Key still in my pocket.
The end of the day its only reward.

I TAKE MY FATHER

Will this one do
with its shadows?
Are doors enough?

On your behalf, a dim hope.

That day, it was cold.
The fish were dead.

The flies.
The key.
The end of day.

RETURN HOME

In the end, no minotaur.
Just the body on the floor.

Weeks later, we searched everywhere.
Ladders up into the attic, flashlights.
Where were the secrets we were looking for?

In the dream, you regret the miracle
I performed, complain about your teeth.

The doors all lead back to the same hallway.
No locks left to pick. It's time to take you
to the condo, downsize your place.
Carry you across the threshold. Welcome you home.
Scatter. Release. Lock. Release. Sleep.

FOR THE FIRST TIME, SNOW

Scent of coming snow

snow body calling me home

calling me post-snow stress disordered

sound of snow falling on snow

you and your mind of winter

without Christmas

without Father

Father of snow and fallen

Foreign snow

Play this where he lies

snow angel

Let it   let it   let it

Let snow be a virtue   let virtue be a silence

Let the house be let

Let snow lead us forward

Let the path lie covered

Let the city stay silent   let silence be virtue

let snow stay until   let spring

GRATITUDE

Several of these poems appeared in print or online:

"Hunt," "Ashore": *Eleven Eleven.*
"Ocean Views," "Dream Development," "The Form of a City": *EVENT.*
"Hole [East, facing West]," "Work in Progress," "My Work in Progress": *Forget.*
"Nearing Winter," "Crow," "Boom Crash Boom Crash": *The Puritan.*
"Realty Check": *Sous Rature.*
"Where I Am" appeared as a broadside with Toronto Poetry Vendors, Spring 2011.
"The Last Waterfront Property" appeared as a No Press pamphlet, Spring 2011.

Thanks to the editors of these fine journals.

"Vancouver Special" formed the basis of projectrebuild.ca, a collaborative poetry project. Many thanks to the poets who became the tenants of this poem, and then built something special of their own from its foundations. Thanks to Starkaður Barkarson for building the site and Marian Churchland for creating the art.

Thanks to the Canada Council for the Arts for time and space to form the words.

Karl Siegler, my editor, built and rebuilt this book with me. Thank you, Karl, for believing in my work, and helping me find the doors in and the windows out.

To the rest of the Talonbooks family, including Gregory Gibson, Garry Thomas Morse, Christy Siegler, and Kevin and Vicki Williams, thank you for bringing this book into being.

Angela Hibbs, Mat Laporte, and a.rawlings, thank you for reading and re-reading.

Thanks to so many for the conversations that wrote these poems, especially Sean Starke. Keith Higgins' vancouverspecial.com was an invaluable resource. I must have borrowed Reg Johanson's insights more than once. Craig Mackie and I sorted out the problems of class, taste, and beauty on more than one occasion. Warren Zahar led me from Surrey to Shangri-La and back again.

There were so many Fridays at Spartacus with the KSW and a community, gathering. Thank you.

To my mother, Monika: so much love.

To my nephew, Judah: take love out of me, put it in you!

Where would I be without my sister, Kimiko, for breathing through all this with me? Too far from Fancytown for my likings. Thank you, SBZ.

Daily gratitude for Denise Dunn. Tim Carson, Heather Curley, Alex Engels, Patrick Greene, Ari Livingstone Sambrano, and the rest of the Lippincott crew: thank you for walking the path with me. Thank you for leading me home.

This book is dedicated to the memory of my father, Yorihide Bruce Murakami, who passed away during its completion, and so changed its shape, and mine.

Sachiko Murakami's first poetry collection, *The Invisibility Exhibit*, was a finalist for the Governer General's Award for Poetry and the Gerald Lampert Memorial Award. She has been a literary worker for various publishers, magazines and organizations, and is a past member of Vancouver's Kootenay School of Writing collective. Born and raised in Vancouver, she lives, for now, in Toronto.